A Canadian Child's Year

HOORAY FOR TODAY!

by Fran Newman and Claudette Boulanger

North Winds Press

A divison of Scholastic-TAB Publications Ltd., Richmond Hill, Ontario, Canada

For Diane, Jeff, Sandra, Tracy, Keri,
Camille, Brendan, Molly,
Kathie, Sandy, Fran, Larry...

design by Kathryn Cole

Published by North Winds Press, a division of Scholastic-TAB Publications Ltd.,
123 Newkirk Rd., Richmond Hill, Ontario, Canada.

Text copyright © 1979 by Fran Newman; illustrations copyright © 1979
by Claudette Boulanger

1st printing 1979

2nd printing 1980   **Printed in Canada**

Canadian Cataloguing in Publication Data

Newman, Fran, 1937-
    Hooray for today!

ISBN 0-590-07623-X

1.Festivals – Canada – Juvenile literature.
I. Boulanger, Claudette, 1940-   II. Title.

GT4813.N45   j394.2'6971   C79-094556-8

To the girls and boys of Canada

What is your favourite day? Your birthday? Hallowe'en?
The last day of school? There are all kinds of days that
we can celebrate. This is a book about "hooray days" —
dates that are special to Canadians in every season
of the year.
    Beginning with Canada's birthday on July 1, you can
enjoy a full year of celebrations that reflect the
cultures and peoples that make up our country. We could
not include them all, of course, but we hope the ones
you find here will give you many more reasons for saying
"hooray for today!" — all year around.

Fran and Claudette

Canada Day

On July 1, 1867, bells rang out from Halifax to Toronto, and the boom of cannons resounded on Parliament Hill. A nation had been born, and all across the new "dominion" people thronged the streets waving flags and rejoicing.

The new country was very largely the dream of Sir John A. Macdonald, who was to become Canada's first prime minister, and Sir George Etienne Cartier, the leader of Lower Canada. From the four weak and disunited colonies of 1867 (New Brunswick, Nova Scotia, Lower Canada and Upper Canada) the country grew and prospered until within a century Canada had spread from Newfoundland to Vancouver Island, from the American border to the North Pole.

Every year on July 1 Canadians of all backgrounds celebrate with joy and thanksgiving the blessings of their country – Sir John A. Macdonald's dream come true.

Sir John's hands gripped the wide lapels of his coat. He drew a deep breath, and stood proud and erect before them.

"Today," he said, "is the First of July. Your country's birthday. A birthday which belongs to us all. For now we are a nation. A nation with the rich heritage of our native peoples and of two cultures, French and English. A nation united. And united we will continue our rapid onward progress under the benign sway of Her Gracious Majesty our Queen."

He paused. His head went back. He spoke out strongly and clearly, as if to invisible listeners far away in space and time.

"And because it belongs to us all, as the years go by, I ask you to remember always what it means. The day of Confederation. The day your country was born." His voice rang. "Never let it be cheapened. Never let it be forgotten or ignored. And honour it always, for it is your country's day!"

Leslie McFarlane

Calgary Stampede

The western plains of Canada and the foothills of the Rockies are the home of a special type of Canadian: the cattleman. Here, knowing how to ride a horse, rope a calf and wrestle down a steer are part of the daily skills of the ranchers. In 1912 some Alberta cattlemen put on a show to display these skills, and that competition has grown into a world-famous event: the Calgary Stampede.

In July of each year, visitors from near and far gather to witness the thrills and excitement of the old and not-so-old West. Cowboys compete against each other in such events as chuckwagon racing and wild-cow milking — and in trying to stay aloft on the back of a wild bucking bronco or a fierce Brahma bull. Clowns add to the fun, but they have a serious job too: to distract the bull from a rider who has been thrown.

In the company of friendly Calgarians, any visitor can feel like a Westerner — and protected from the sun by a magnificent white stetson, can definitely feel "home on the range."

The first Calgary Stampede in 1912 was seven days of thrills and spills — with most of the thrills and spills being provided by a snorting, spinning, wild-eyed bundle of black dynamite called "Cyclone." As the show moved into its final day, Cyclone's record was intact. A total of 129 men had tried to mount him and stay on him, and 129 men had ended up in the dust.

The crowd cheered when the announcer gave the word that Tom Three Persons, a young Indian cowboy from MacLeod, was about to ride. But the cheers gave way to groans when he added that Tom would be climbing on the back of Cyclone.

The Calgary Herald recorded the scene: "Bucking, twisting, swapping ends and resorting to every artifice of the outlaw, Cyclone swept across the field. The Indian was jarred from one side to the other, but as the crowd cheered themselves hoarse he settled every time into the saddle and waited for the next lurch or twist.

"His bucking unable to dislodge the rider, Cyclone stood at rest and reared straight up. Once it looked as though Tom was to follow the fate of his predecessors. He recovered rapidly and from that time forward Cyclone bucked till he was tired. The Indian had mastered him!"

Jacques Hamilton

Highland Games

It has been said that Canada is the child of the Scots and the French. The Scots took up the great task of exploring the continent which the French had begun – and everywhere the Scots went, their bagpipes went with them. The skirl of the pipes echoed down empty rivers and through lonely forest clearings as sturdy Scottish factors built the vast network of the Hudson's Bay Company. And whenever Canadians have gone to war, they have stirred to the brave summons of the pipes.

Today Canadians of Scottish and non-Scottish background love to take part in the regional Scottish festivals, where the old skills and games – highland dancing, caber tossing and hammer throwing – are still proudly displayed. And no one can resist the thrilling spectacle of tartan-clad pipe bands competing against each other. One of the most important Games is held in Antigonish, Nova Scotia. Thousands visit it every year – and go home with the strains of "Scotland the Brave" still ringing in their ears.

MacTavish fingered his bagpipe chanter, and asked the owl to hoot again. So MacOwl hootled while MacTavish piped, and the hootling and tootling blended together to produce the most amazing music. Angus Dugal MacTavish marched up and down the length of the room playing his chanter with all his might, while Great Horned MacOwl marched around and around the kitchen table top and hootled with all his heart.

Mr. MacTavish ran out of breath just about the time when MacOwl ran out of hootles. Regretfully, the man laid aside his pipes and said, "A-weel, Ah havna felt sae contented-like for a lang, lang time, but Ah mustna neglect ma wurrrk. There's ma sheep tae mind an' ma neeps tae hoe."

MacOwl nodded his understanding and said, "Aye, an' for masel', Ah must gan awa' an' look fer my family an' help them alang wi' the hoolet business."

Angus MacTavish asked, "But wull ye no' come back again?"

MacOwl said, "Och, Ah wis hopin' ye'd ask me back."

"Come ony time ye like, freend – an' whenever ye do come, mayhap we'll ha'e oorselves a wee bit o'music tae keep us in fine feckle."

"Aye, we'll do juist that," said MacOwl.

Kerry Wood

Caribana

Canadians of African descent have played an important part in Canada's development since the early days of English Canada. Thousands came north as Loyalists to escape the American revolutionaries. Others found freedom in the days before the American Civil War by taking the "underground railway" to Canada. In recent years thousands more have come from the sunny Caribbean.

Whenever black Canadians gather, they reveal their special gifts for music and colour and dance. One of the most spectacular gatherings is held in Toronto in August. The downtown streets and the parkland spaces of nearby Centre Island ring to the music of steel bands, calypso songs (like the traditional *Tinga-lay-o*) and the shouts and laughter of happy people. Children and adults dress up in dazzling costumes for the yearly parade. Canadians of many cultures join in the fun – and when darkness finally settles over Centre Island, the spirit of Caribana lingers on.

My donkey hee, my donkey haw,
My donkey sleep in a bed of straw,
My donkey short, my donkey wide,
Don't get too close to his backside.

Tinga-lay-o, run my little donkey run,
Tinga-lay-o, run my little donkey run.

My donkey walk, my donkey talk,
My donkey eat with a knife and fork;
My donkey eat, my donkey sleep,
My donkey kick with his two hind feet.

I go out to play, my neighbour she say,
"Take all your friends and you go away."
I say, "It's true, you belong in the zoo
'Cause all of the monkeys they look like you."

My teacher mad, my teacher sad,
'Cause all the little children are acting so bad;
The pencil fly, hit my teacher in the eye,
And now my poor teacher she start to cry.

You can sing this slow, you can sing this fast,
You can sing this sitting on the grass;
You can sing this slow, you can sing this fast,
You can sing this sitting on the grass.

Traditional

Labour Day

The first Monday in September is a date which reminds everyone that summer is coming to an end. But summer does not end quietly. On the West Coast, people throng to the great Pacific National Exhibition where, in addition to all the excitement of the midway, the annual logging show takes place. In Central Canada it is the Canadian National Exhibition, with its air show and hundreds of displays and rides, that draws millions of visitors. And in many other communities across the country similar, though smaller, fairs and festivals take place.

Labour Day was first declared a public holiday in 1894 to honour Canada's labour associations. Since that time it has become a day on which all Canadians – particularly the young – celebrate the last holiday weekend before the new school term, and prepare for the arrival of brisker autumn weather.

World's fairs were events we'd heard of – one of the things I remember was a walking stick made of clear pale-blue twisted glass that hung from the plate rail in our dining room, a souvenir of the St. Louis World's Fair, where my mother and father had gone on their honeymoon. "Meet Me in St. Louis, Louis," which became popular at that time, was one of the songs my mother used to sing waltzing around the kitchen with the dishcloth and occasionally with my father.

But World's Fairs seemed, to us kids, to be rather show-off affairs that happened in unreal parts of the world. The real event, as permanent and dependable as falling leaves, was the C.N.E., which we felt everybody from remote places like California wanted to see. We sometimes pictured them sitting around their supper tables talking about it and envying us, and you couldn't blame them, for we kids lived within a streetcar ride of it and could go every day if we could afford the fifteen cents' admission.

Robert Thomas Allen

Thanksgiving

When the Pilgrims landed in America in 1621 they found a rich and fertile land. And when their first harvest was gathered in, they gave special thanks for their good fortune. Their Canadian descendants, too, set aside one day in the year to give special recognition to the blessings of their land.

All across Canada families gather on the second Monday in October to celebrate the joys of family life and good food. And what food! Roast turkey, cranberry sauce, fresh green peas, mashed potatoes and rich brown gravy, followed by pumpkin pie – and ice cream if you have room for it!

Even in the age of supermarkets and refrigeration, in the quiet moments that follow Thanksgiving dinner families sense the gratitude and satisfaction of the pioneers when the harvest was safely stored – the gift of abundance, and proof against the stern winter months ahead.

Your crop is in against the winter. As you store it away; as you cunningly braid your onions upon their suspended strings; as you wheelbarrow the squashes from the garden like a parent wheeling a baby, to avoid the danger of shock; as you pick the apples from the tree, fondling each to prevent bruises; as the last potato is safely lifted from the earth, you know how your grandfather felt when the log barn and underground root cellar were full.

The true farmers are laying in the last of their crop now, from the tiny fishing farms of Nova Scotia to the apple valley of the Okanagan and the lush delta of the Fraser River. The countryman is heaping up his woodpile. Every small boy is examining his skates in the basement. People are wondering where they stored their skis during the summer. In the mountains the railway men are looking to the snowsheds, and on the prairies to the snow fences.

Bruce Hutchinson

Oktoberfest

Many Canadians trace their families back with pride to the rugged German-speaking Pennsylvania Dutch who were among the first Loyalists to carve out new homes in the wilderness that was then Ontario. Others look back to the skilful craftsmen of Lunenburg, Nova Scotia, whose descendants built the famous *Bluenose* seen on the back of nearly every dime.

Where there are German-Canadian communities, whether of ancient or recent origin, there is a special time of year when all work ceases and people turn to the pleasures of singing and dancing, eating marvellous food, and celebrating *gemütlichkeit* with oceans of German beer. This is Oktoberfest, which began as a wedding celebration in 1810 and grew into an annual "worldwide" Bavarian festival.

In Kitchener-Waterloo, Ontario, a favourite spectacle is the parade. Included among its colourful floats is a magnificent beer wagon drawn by a team of beautiful Belgian horses that step proudly to the strains of an oompah band.

My grandfather's hand is tightly around mine, reassuring to a little boy in such a crowd. Would I like candy-floss, he asks, or Turkish honey? Or maybe a bite of one of those chickens browning on a spit over glowing embers? The scent of herrings-in-buns competes with the smell of sausages, pretzels and licorice. Finally the sweet aroma of honey-almonds roasting in a copper kettle wins out. They're crunchy, and oh, so good!

The slide. Up the tower I go. Whoosh! my carpet speeds me faster and faster to the bottom where my grandfather catches me. It sure is nice to have a grandad.

We walk on. It's getting dark now and thousands of coloured lights blink and glare. Are those birds I hear? No, a man on a chair is making the sounds with a paper no bigger than a nickel pressed against his tongue. I try and try, but all I do is make a squeak as the paper pops out of my mouth.

We go into the beer-tent. Inside are thousands of people around wooden tables, singing, arms locked into arms, swaying from side to side to the music of the brass band …

Grandfather must have carried me home. I remember waking up next morning still dreaming of my day at Oktoberfest.

Horst Schmid

Hallowe'en

From the earliest days, people in the British Isles paid special attention to a shivery time of year when ghosts and goblins, witches and spooks, black cats and skeletons roamed the countryside. In Christian tradition it became All Hallows Eve, the night when the spirits of the damned returned to Earth. To be safe, householders put out gifts of wine and food so that unwelcome visitors would not do them mischief. In Ireland, Jack-o'-lanterns made of pumpkins or turnips were used to scare away evil spirits.

On October 31, in nearly every town in Canada, the tradition goes on. Monsters and witches take to the streets, but instead of seeking gifts from doorsteps, they hammer on doors shouting, "Trick or treat!" Frightened homeowners have no choice but to give them what they want: candy, nuts, apples, chewing gum and homemade cookies. This goes on till late at night when weary spooks are seen staggering home with heavy bags.

Dessert forgotten, the whole family trooped to the door. Outside four boys waited, one dressed as a skeleton. Meg "Oo-oo-ed" at the sight of him. Kent knew all the others in spite of their costumes, but the skeleton had him stumped.

"You're Mark? Victor? Sammy?" Kent tried, peering at what little could be seen of the boy beneath the bones. They were painted in white on a black suit that covered him from head to heel.

Each time the skeleton denied the charge, answering first in the voice of a little old lady, then a small boy, then a giggly girl.

All at once, Kent cried, "I know! You're Rusty Sardis! Your Dad painted those bones on you. He's a doctor!"

"Rusty!" squeaked the skeleton. "Who's he? Never heard of him!"

Kent danced around, knowing he'd guessed right.

Jean Little

Remembrance Day

More than once in her first century Canada went to war to defend the rights and values on which she herself was built. In World War I more than 600,000 Canadians joined in the terrible struggle to free France and Belgium. 60,000 of those soldiers died – many of them buried "in Flander's Fields." A generation later, when Europe was occupied by the Nazis, Canadian armies again crossed the Atlantic. On August 19, 1942, one of the most tragic encounters of the war took place. A force of 5,000 Canadians was sent to test German defences in a daring sea raid on Dieppe, Normandy. The enemy was prepared – French and English Canadians died together under a murderous hail of fire. The survivors went into three miserable years of captivity.

   On November 11, Canadians remember with pride and sorrow the young men and women of all the wars who so freely laid down their lives so that others might live in peace and dignity.

This was my brother
At Dieppe,
Quietly a hero
Who gave his life
Like a gift,
Withholding nothing.

His youth…his love…
His enjoyment of being alive…
His future, like a book
With half the pages still uncut –

This was my brother
At Dieppe…
The one who built me a doll house
When I was seven,
Complete to the last small picture frame,
Nothing forgotten.

He was awfully good at fixing things,
At stepping into the breach when he was needed.

That's what he did at Dieppe;
He was needed.
And even death must have been a little ashamed
At his eagerness!

Mona Gould

Grey Cup

Once a year, on a cool late November weekend, Canada splits into two hostile camps. It has nothing to do with politics or language – and everything to do with whether one's roots and sympathies lie east or west of the Ontario-Manitoba border. It is Grey Cup weekend, when the top teams from East and West face each other with fierce determination to carry off Canadian football's highest trophy: the Grey Cup.

Earl Grey liked to slip away from his duties as governor-general to watch rugby football at Ottawa's Varsity Oval. In 1909 he donated a cup to be awarded to the "amateur champions of Canada." It was not until 1921 that the first East-West game took place. Since then the annual confrontation has grown to be a national event watched on millions of television sets from coast to coast.

With only seconds remaining in the 1960 Grey Cup at Vancouver (Ottawa 16, Edmonton 6), an exuberant fan romped out between the teams, picked up the ball and ran off with it – something the team players had been trying to do all afternoon.

The invader made it look quite simple. He slipped into No Man's Land between the teams, picked up the ball lying in front of the centre – who was standing upright awaiting the call to the huddle – and ran off with it as players and officials gazed aghast.

This triggered a downpour of 5,000 other exuberants from the stands. That ended the game, despite forty-one unplayed seconds showing on the big clock.

Andy O'Brien

Hanukkah

Many of the celebrations of Jewish family life commemorate events that took place in the Jewish people's long and heroic history. The Hebrew word "Hanukkah" means "dedication" and recalls a miracle that took place more than 2,000 years ago. A Syrian king had closed the Jewish Temple and destroyed the scrolls of the Torah. A brave family called the Maccabees rallied their people and expelled the Syrians, but when they came to rededicate the Temple, there was only enough oil for one day. Even so, the lamps continued to burn for eight full days!

Today the miracle is recalled in a December festival that lasts eight days. Each day a new candle is lit in the eight-branched Menorah. Relatives gather for special prayers and to exchange gifts. Children receive *Hanukkah gelt* (money), play games with *draidls* (square-sided spinning tops) and feast on Hanukkah delicacies. It is a time of rededication and joyous family life — symbolized by the brightly glowing candles placed in the window of each home.

The eve of Hanukkah, brittle-cold, with the sun swiftly descending almost at midday. Inside the house on Dufferin Avenue, excitement was quickly building. The children could hardly contain themselves with the prospect of getting dressed up, the whole family going to Fetter Leib's house for the lighting of the first candle…

A hush as people crowded into the not-very-large living room, the overspill staying in the hall. Rachel, as a newcomer, was privileged to be up close to watch her father-in-law light a match and hold it to the wick in the scooped-out potato filled with oil. His voice rang out with the Hanukkah blessings and her heart filled with joy. How beautifully he sang!

And now everyone wished everyone else a *"Gutta Hanukkah,"* and before the noise could get completely out of hand, Fetter Leib assembled them all for the annual ritual which, even though he was not a rich man, he had long ago established: each child had to come forward and receive Fetter Leib's blessings and eighteen cents, which was *chai* (life), and every adult, no matter what age, must receive a quarter.

Bess Kaplan

Christmas Eve

Near Midland, Ontario, stands a tiny settlement surrounded by a high log palisade. It is a reconstruction of Sainte-Marie among the Hurons, founded by two of Canada's early martyrs: Father Jean de Brébeuf and Father Gabriel Lalemant. These two men brought Christianity to the Hurons in 1626 and twenty-three years later, at the hands of invading Iroquois, suffered a terrible death for their faith.

Brébeuf recognized that the story of Jesus had to be conveyed to his Huron congregation in terms they would understand. So he wrote a carol, "Jesus Ahatonhia," proclaiming the miraculous story of Christmas, using the Huron language and the Huron experience.

Although the Iroquois wars scattered and almost destroyed the Hurons, the hymn lived on in their tradition. A hundred years later another Jesuit missionary copied the words down, and these in turn were translated into English. Now Father Jean de Brébeuf's beautiful carol is part of the heritage not only of Indian Christians but of Christians all across Canada.

'Twas in the moon of winter time when all the birds had fled,
That Mighty Gitchi Manitou sent angel choirs instead.
Before their light the stars grew dim,
And wand'ring hunters heard the hymn.

"Jesus, your King, is born;
Jesus is born;
In Excelsis Gloria!"

Within a lodge of broken bark the tender Babe was found.
A ragged robe of rabbit skin enwrapped His beauty 'round.
And as the hunter braves drew nigh,
The angel song rang loud and high.

The earliest moon of winter time is not so round and fair,
As was the ring of glory on the helpless Infant there.
While Chiefs from far before Him knelt,
With gifts of fox and beaver pelt.

O children of the forest free, O sons of Manitou,
The Holy Child of earth and heav'n is born today for you.
Come, kneel before the radiant Boy,
Who brings you beauty, peace and joy.

Father Jean de Brébeuf

Christmas

From pioneer times to the present, Christmas has always been the most wonderful time of the year. The day begins early – sometimes before light – with an excited descent on the presents heaped under the sparkling Christmas tree. Amid mountains of wrapping paper and shiny new toys, time-out is called for Christmas breakfast, and perhaps a church service.

Later in the day there is Christmas dinner, sometimes at Grandma and Grandpa's house, where aunts and uncles, cousins and friends may be present for the great feast. And what a feast! Golden-brown turkey, glazed ham with pineapple and cherries, roast potatoes and heaps of vegetables. Then comes dessert: pies and trifle and plum pudding with a choice of sauces!

In every corner of Canada, from isolated farmhouses to big cities, on this day people discover anew the joys of family and fellowship. Finally it is time to say goodbye, zip up snowsuits and head for home. Another Christmas has ended – the best ever.

Too soon the day was over. Elmer and I huddled snug in our beds. Outside, the night sky blazed with northern lights. The howl of coyotes, so terrifying when we first came west, was almost comforting now. They were part of the prairie, and the prairie was good to us.

That first Christmas had reaffirmed for me the values I was learning day by day: the warmth of family, the loyalty of friends, the special kind of goodwill that reaches out to those less fortunate. These are the important things, I was beginning to realize. It was a good lesson for living, and a good thought to fall asleep with, on that happiest of Christmas nights.

John Diefenbaker

New Year's Eve

Cars honk, noisemakers bray, and up and down the streets shouts of merriment burst out. It is midnight, and everywhere doors are thrown open to offer a happy welcome to the New Year. Then, as the minute hand moves past twelve, the merrymakers retreat to the warmth of their living rooms to reaffirm the good things of the past year. Arm-in-arm they sing a heartfelt "Auld Lang Syne."

From the early days of history, the end of the old year and the beginning of the new have had special importance. In nearly every society it has been a time to take stock of the past and to hope for (and plan) better things for the year ahead. The joyful party which goes on into the wee hours is followed by more sober thoughts and "resolutions."

Although in Canada the day-long social round of pioneer times noted by Susanna Moodie has disappeared, it is still a time for telephone calls to family and friends to offer sincerest wishes for "the very best the year can bring."

On New-Year's day all the gentlemen in the place call upon their friends, to wish them a happy New Year, and to exchange friendly greetings with the ladies of the family, who are always in readiness to receive them, and make them a return for these marks of neighbourly regard, in the substantial form of rich cakes, fruit, wine, coffee, and tea. It is generally a happy, cheerful day; all faces wear a smile, old quarrels are forgotten, and everyone seems anxious to let ill-will and heart-burnings die with the old year.

It is an especial frolic for all the lads who have just returned from school or college to enjoy their Christmas holidays. Cakes and sweetmeats are showered upon them in abundance, and they feel themselves of vast importance, while paying their compliments to the ladies, and running from house to house, with their brief congratulatory address – "I wish you all a happy New Year!"

Susanna Moodie

Chinese New Year

Chinese civilization is the oldest in the world. And Chinese Canadians, whether descended from the men who built the transcontinental railways or from more recent arrivals, still maintain the old traditions.

One of the most important is the New Year celebration. It begins with the new moon in January and lasts until the moon is full. It is a time of renewal and rejoicing. Gifts and greetings are exchanged, special foods are prepared, and relatives and friends visit each other. In the first days there is a Lion Dance: performers wearing a lion costume prance in the streets, accompanied by musicians and dancers. Later comes the spectacular Dragon Dance. Sometimes as many as thirty men leap and sway in a long red and gold dragon skin with a huge papier-mâché head, to frighten away any evil spirits left over from the old year. Firecrackers explode and paper lanterns swing as the happy throng follows the dragon. Finally it is all over – and everyone returns home knowing the year is off to a splendid start.

My parents made sure that we were clean and neatly dressed, and that the house was in the best of order. Fresh fruit, Chinese sweetmeats and a *chuen-hap* of preserved fruits were on hand. All was ready for the relatives and close friends who would come to help us greet the New Year.

After lunch, mother and father took us downtown to watch the Lion Dance, a visit by the Chinese Lion to all the stores and downtown establishments. Firecrackers rattled off everywhere, symbolically to drive away evil and bring good luck and prosperity to all. What a spectacular event – the clash of symbols and gongs, and a prancing gold, red and white "lion" manned by the local Chinese Athletic Association!

Later that evening we visited relatives, calling *"Gung Hay Sun Nien"* when we arrived. Year by year, we children seemed to accumulate more elders – uncles, aunts, grand-uncles, great-grand-uncles, great-aunts – and every one of them gave us a *lai-sih,* a small red envelope with money that we could spend or save.

That night when mother tucked me in, I thought about what a wonderful thing *Sun Nien* really was. Too bad it came only once a year!

Ying Hope

Carnaval

What brings together the fun and excitement of winter sports, the traditional hospitality of Québec and the colourful festivities of Mardi Gras? The Québec winter carnival, of course – Carnaval!

In 1955 some imaginative Québec businessmen decided the city needed something to break the monotony of midwinter. The result was a festival symbolized by the giant snowman (nearly two metres) called "Bonhomme Carnaval." Clad in a red-buttoned snow coat, a jaunty tuque and a brightly coloured *ceinture fléchée* Bonhomme Carnaval presides over a host of events packed together into ten lively days in February.

Among these are the ice slide down the promenade steps, an ice sculpture contest, a peewee hockey tournament, parades, dancing in the streets, a soapbox derby, snowmobile races, and finally a thrilling canoe race across the ice floes of the St. Lawrence. It all ends with a Mardi Gras parade, a splendid ball at the Château Frontenac – and lots of happy memories for the thousands of visitors who attended Carnaval.

The old capital is liveliest in winter during the carnival…when the city is ruled by the carnival snowman and the newly elected carnival queen. Then a fairy ice palace is built on the hill facing the Quebec Parliament; people dance in the streets and – to warm themselves – drink liquor from the popular red and white canes.

In the Saint-Sauveur district, visitors come from all over to admire the ice sculpture along the sidewalks of Sainte-Thérèse Street: a marvellous exhibition of dinosaur monsters, fat women, boats from the ice race, famous people, and all kinds of animals, beautiful and grotesque. This fantasy world becomes really weird at night when all the sculptures are brilliantly lit by thousands of lamps.

Miyuki Tanobe
From QUEBEC JE T'AIME I LOVE YOU © 1976 Miyuki Tanobe, published by Tundra Books.

Valentine's Day

People change and festivals change, and often new meanings are given to old symbols. A century ago, valentines were special greetings offered by young men to the ones they hoped to marry. Now they have become symbols of love and friendship – to be sent to anyone who is really special. Although no one can be sure when the tradition began, the name Valentine is associated with two saints who were martyred for their faith. One was a young man who died February 14, A.D. 270. Legend tells us he left a farewell note to his jailer's little daughter – and signed it "From your Valentine."

Valentine symbols include red hearts, lacy frills, cupids – and often little poems. As February approaches each year, there is a great demand for red construction paper and pretty paper doilies as young fingers create their special greetings. A few lucky ones will be able to mail their cards from Love, Saskatchewan, or Heart's Desire, Newfoundland. But anywhere in Canada, a valentine can be delivered just as well by hand.

my friend is like bark
rounding a tree

she warms like sun
on a winter day

she cools like water
in the hot noon

her voice is ready
as a spring bird

she is my friend
and I am hers

Emily Hearn

Arctic Winter Games

Southern Canadians find it hard to think of sports and games in the harsh climate of the Far North and during the six months of Arctic darkness, but among the Inuit, games have always played an important part in everyday life. As Inuit life changed, many of the traditional pastimes were in danger of being lost — but now they have made a dramatic comeback.

Every two years since 1970, athletes from all parts of Northern and Arctic Canada have gathered to compete in one of the most spectacular and varied sporting events in North America — the Arctic Winter Games. Side by side with such familiar athletic contests as basketball and judo are found traditional Inuit pastimes like knuckle hopping, precision whip flicking and walrus-hide tossing. The illustration shows an athlete trying to kick a sealskin ball hanging from a pole in a game called *agraorak*. At the Arctic Games, modern children of the North enjoy the best of both worlds in a thrilling week-long festival.

Sometimes in the winter it was boring in the igloo but we never stayed inside much. The fathers would make toy sleds for their sons and daughters to slide on and, when the children had their sleds and their toy whips, they would play outside most of the day.

Very often in those days when we felt happy in camp, Ashoona and I would play the accordion. My favourite brother once gave me an accordion and we both could play. The little children would come and dance.

We played lots of games. One game was *illupik* — jumping over the *avatuk,* the sealskin float that hunters used to tie to the harpoons so the seals would stay on the water after they were killed.

Another game was tennis! This is how we played this game — we threw a ball underhand and tried to catch it in a sealskin racket. The racket was called an *autuk.* We made the ball from caribou skin and stuffed it with something. We used to play this game a lot, even in winter. It was a good game, but they don't play it now; they are following the world.

Pitseolak

St. Patrick's Day

Ireland's gifts to the world are countless. Among them are laughter, music and the ability to tell tall tales that would render the angels speechless with amazement. Irishmen have left their mark in Canada in the names of towns and counties, and in the lighthearted jigs that set toes tapping at barn dances. Regardless of background, Canadians agree that "everyone's an Irishman on St. Patrick's Day." Father wears a green tie, mother a green dress — and children delight in making shamrock cookies with green icing.

Little is known about the saint himself, but a host of legends have come down through the ages since his death on March 17, A.D.493: that he chased poisonous snakes out of Ireland, that he lit a fire of snow and that he used the shamrock to demonstrate the Holy Trinity. What is known is that his eloquence and gentle nature made him beloved throughout the Emerald Isle. It would be nice to think that some of these lovely blessings sprang from the lips of St. Patrick himself.

Here are a few Irish blessings that you might like to toss off when the spirit moves you:

May God speed you on your way and see you safe home.

May God and His Holy Mother take the harm of the year away from you.

May the roads rise to meet you,
may the wind be always at your back,
may the sun shine warm upon your face,
the rains fall softly upon your fields,
and until we meet again,
may God hold you in the palm of his hand.

But the loveliest one I've ever heard goes like this:

May the blessed sunlight shine upon you,
and warm your heart until it glows like a great fire,
so that a stranger may come and warm himself at it,
and also a friend.

If you can't quite pull that one off, you can always say *Irish luck to you* or *God spare you the health* and leave it at that.

Helen FitzPatrick

Easter

When the first great Ukrainian immigration to the West took place in the 1890's, the settlers found a land very similar to the one they had left behind: great fertile plains under a vast and beautiful sky. Soon the new land and the ancient Ukrainian culture had combined to create a marvellously rich addition to Canadian life.

Of all the arts the Ukrainian settlers brought, none captured the imagination of other Canadians as much as the intricately decorated eggs called *pysanky*. These are made every Easter and combine the most joyful Christian message with an art form that began thousands of years ago to celebrate the return of spring. According to Ukrainian legend, as long as pysanky are made, goodness will prevail over evil.

At Vegreville, Alberta, visiting children who are more accustomed to chocolate eggs can see the most amazing pysanka in the world: a huge multicoloured monument that proclaims the message of joy and love all year round.

Mother taught us girls how to decorate Easter eggs. She didn't make them too fancy, just very simple. As long as there was a line around and some leaf. You see, they believed very much in all that from the old country. The line that encircles the egg has no beginning or end so it symbolizes eternity. And a pine tree, she always made a pine tree to signify eternal youth and health. She made roosters, eternity and fulfilment of wishes, and always a fish for Christianity. Mother never made reindeers, but other people did. They must have come from a different village. The dyes were all from the old country, beautiful dyes.

Myrna Kostash

Stanley Cup

"He shoots! He scores!" In the days of radio, the voice of the famous broadcaster Foster Hewitt carried the Stanley Cup playoffs into nearly every home in Canada. Since then, the popularity of the game that began on the frozen lakes of Canada has spread around the world.

The high point of the hockey year comes each spring when the best teams of the National Hockey League compete in the playoffs for the Stanley Cup – and the nation follows with furious attention.

The cup was donated in 1893 by Governor-General Lord Stanley who was a keen hockey fan and whose eight sons played on a local team. Since then, the silver cup (which cost $48.66) has been booted into the Rideau Canal, used as a flowerpot, forgotten on a roadside and stolen several times. To protect it, a copy was made (costing $14,000) and the real Stanley Cup now rests securely in a bank vault.

Maurice Richard's goal on April 8, 1952, is said to be the most sensational goal in NHL history. The scene was the Montreal Forum and the Canadiens were playing Detroit in the semifinal round for the Stanley Cup. In the second period of the seventh game Maurice ran into a shuddering body check – and came to in the sick bay while the team doctor was putting the last six stitches in his head. The Rocket sat out the remainder of that period and sixteen minutes of the last one, but with the score tied, he refused to be kept on the bench.

When he came on the ice the fans raised the roof. At centre ice Bouchard laid a pass on Richard's stick as he passed in full flight. Richard turned and swooped across the centre line, dodged past two Detroit players, crossed the blue line and swerved to the right as if making for the corner. Another turn, then he cut across the goal mouth… The shot was so fast the goalkeeper wouldn't have seen it if he'd been looking. All he could do was fish it out of the net.

Montreal went on to win the Cup that year, and Maurice added another story to the Richard legend.

Bobby Hull

Victoria Day

Queen Victoria was one of Canada's most beloved sovereigns. Her birthday, May 24, became a holiday with firework displays and public celebrations. In 1898, the day before her birthday was declared Empire Day and school children across Canada honoured the great family of nations over which the Queen reigned. At the end of the Empire Day ceremonies children would chant:

The 24th of May
Is the Queen's birthday.
If you don't give us a holiday,
We'll all run away
And hide behind the old bobsleigh.

When Queen Victoria died in 1901 after a reign of sixty-four years, it seemed impossible that she was really gone. So the holiday and the fireworks remained – and although the day officially celebrates the birthday of the reigning monarch, it continues to be "Victoria Day."

In Québec, May 24 is called Dollard des Ormeaux Day, after the heroic leader of a small band who in 1649 gave their lives to save Montréal from destruction.

On our street, summer officially arrived on the twenty-fourth of May in a wonderful wave of gassy smells, from gunpowder, burning punk, and fireworks. Just before dark, families came out onto their verandas and there was a general rustling around the houses as one appointed expert in each family arranged milk bottles to launch skyrockets and opened paper bags of pinwheels, stone crackers, lawn lights, and Roman candles as hard as broom handles, and waited for the sky to get dark.

This was all in celebration of Queen Victoria's birthday, although we kids didn't know it. When we beat our schoolbooks, chanting "Twenty-fourth of May, the Queen's birthday," it was pure exuberance at being let out of school for a day. Queen Victoria reigned long before us, yet not long enough ago for us to study in history.

Next day we kids went around in the pale sunlight picking up burnt skyrockets and trying to find firecrackers that hadn't exploded, recapturing some of the magic of departed glories.

Robert Thomas Allen

St. Antony's Day

Italian people have had a long and proud association with Canada. It was an Italian, Giovanni Caboto (John Cabot), who in 1497 first claimed North America for England. And four hundred years later the Italian scientist Marconi sent the first wireless message across the Atlantic from Newfoundland. Today, Italian communities can be found across Canada – and wherever they are located, Italian old-country skills and hard work have made a lasting contribution to Canadian life.

Italian Canadians maintain many of the festivals of their homeland. One of the most popular is the Feast of St. Antony of Padua, the saint who takes special care of children. His day, June 13 (or the nearest Sunday), is a day for religious and family celebrations. After the parade there is often a joyful community picnic with mounds of delicious Italian food and special games and prizes for the children.

The ringing of the church bells was the signal for the procession to start, and for the Perfetti brothers to set off their smoke and noise bombs. The band struck up a brisk march, and through the huge doors emerged four men bedecked with sashes of red, white and green, the colours of the Italian flag. Each man gripped a handle of the litter which supported a painted statue of the saint.

From a second-storey balcony across the narrow street, Maria D'Alonzo appeared, dressed as an angel, a sturdy leather harness attached to a pulley hidden under her winged gold and white costume. She rode a wire cable high above the parade to waiting arms in a window of the church choir loft. She clutched a basket under her arm and showered the saint with flowers and *confetti* (pink and white Italian candies with almonds in the middle). She kept her eyes shut ever so tightly. All us kids admired Maria, but we knew she was no angel.

Following the band and the various societies with their flags, sashes and medals, came children dressed in monks' brown habits, the boys with their heads shaved like St. Antony's. As the statue of the saint went by, parents prodded their children to go forward and pin money on the ribbons. These were donations for the church, to thank St. Antony for favours received.

Carlo Italiano

St. Jean Baptiste Day

Samuel de Champlain is called the Father of New France, but his example and his vision for Canada are cherished by both French- and English-speaking Canadians alike. Champlain established the first permanent French settlement on the St. Lawrence in 1608 – and it was his determination that kept the little colony alive over a lifetime of struggle.

Today the province that bears the name of that settlement, Québec, honours Champlain's dream of French civilization in North America each June 24. That is St. Jean Baptiste Day, the day Champlain's Recollet missionaries celebrated their first Mass on Canadian soil. In former years parades were held in Montréal depicting the history and heroes of French Canada. The highlight was the appearance of St. Jean himself, played by a small blond boy holding a white lamb. More recently the celebrations have become less elaborate: dancing in the streets, and at night, huge festive bonfires. But no matter how it is celebrated, Champlain's dream lives on – in Québec and all across Canada.

It may also be said that the country of New France is a new world and not a kingdom, being perfectly beautiful, with very suitable sites on the banks of the great river St. Lawrence (the country's ornament) and on other rivers, lakes, ponds and streams, with an infinite number of beautiful islands, having on them very pleasant and delightful meadows and groves, in which in spring and summer one sees a great number of birds which come there in their time and season. The soil is very fertile for all sorts of grain; there are pastures in abundance and a network of great rivers and lakes which are like seas, covering the country, and which lend a great facility to all the explorations into the interior, whence one may proceed to the western, eastern, and northern oceans and even into the south.

The country is covered with great, tall forests full of all the same varieties of trees we have in France; the air is healthy and the waters excellent along the same parallels of latitude as ours; and the benefit to be derived from this country, as the Sieur de Champlain hopes to show, is quite sufficient to make the matter worthy of consideration, since this country can yield for the King's service the same advantages we enjoy in France.

Samuel de Champlain

Contributors

Robert Thomas Allen

Robert Thomas Allen is a Toronto freelance writer and novelist. Of his many books, two have won the Stephen Leacock Award for Humour, and another has received a Governor-General's Award. The two excerpts are from *My Childhood and Yours, Memories of Growing Up,* reprinted by permission of The Macmillan Company of Canada Limited.

Jean de Brébeuf

Father Jean de Brébeuf (1593-1649) was canonized in 1930. He wrote the first dictionary and grammar of the Huron language, as well as several religious works. "Jesus Ahatonhia" is reprinted by permission of the copyright owner, The Frederick Harris Music Company Limited, Oakville, Canada.

Samuel de Champlain

Samuel de Champlain (1570-1635) became Governor of New France in 1633. He wrote extensively of his travels through the new country. The excerpt first appeared in *Les Voyages,* printed in Paris in 1632. It is reprinted from *The Works of Samuel de Champlain,* vol. 3, edited by H.P. Biggar, by permission of The Champlain Society, Toronto.

John Diefenbaker

One of Canada's best-loved political leaders, John Diefenbaker (1895-1979) moved to the West when he was a young boy. He became leader of the Saskatchewan Conservative Party in 1936 and was Prime Minister of Canada from 1957 to 1963. "My First Prairie Christmas" originally appeared in *Reader's Digest,* December, 1976. The excerpt is reprinted by permission of Reader's Digest Magazines Ltd.

Helen FitzPatrick

Helen FitzPatrick, an Alberta freelance writer and photographer, is a regular contributor to a number of Canadian and American periodicals. The piece about Irish blessings is adapted from "Irish Blessings and a Few Curses, Too," which first appeared in Alberta's *Heritage* magazine, March-April, 1978. It is reprinted by permission of the author.

Mona Gould

Mona Gould sold her first poem when she was only ten years old. She started her career in journalism, then spent several years in radio. She has published two poetry collections: *Tasting the Earth* and *I Run With a Fox.* "This Was My Brother" is from *Tasting the Earth,* reprinted by permission of The Macmillan Company of Canada Limited.

Jacques Hamilton

Jacques Hamilton is a widely published freelance writer whose work has appeared in many daily newspapers. The excerpt from "Taming the Cyclone" is adapted from *People,* one of the *Our Alberta Heritage* series. It is reprinted by permission of Calgary Power Ltd.

Emily Hearn

A full-time script writer for school radio broadcasts, Emily Hearn has also worked for the NFB and the CBC. She loves to write poetry, and several of her poems have appeared in readers and anthologies. "My Friend" is from *Hockey Cards & Hopscotch,* © 1971, adapted and reprinted by permission of Thomas Nelson & Sons (Canada) Limited.

Ying Hope

Ying Hope is a Toronto alderman, and a prominent member of the city's large Chinese community. He has been actively involved in local events and municipal politics for a number of years. The selection describing the Chinese New Year was written especially for *Hooray For Today!* © 1979 by Ying Hope.

Bobby Hull

One of Canada's best-known hockey stars, Bobby Hull started playing professionally at the age of eighteen, and since then has had a long and outstanding career in the NHL and WHA hockey leagues. The excerpt is adapted from "The Most Sensational Goal in NHL History" in *Hockey Is My Game.* It is reprinted by permission of the author.

Bruce Hutchinson

For many years a journalist for the *Victoria Times,* Bruce Hutchinson has written several books and a number of short stories. He has won three Governor-General's Awards for his books about Canada and Canadians. The excerpt is from *Western Windows,* reprinted by permission of Academic Press Canada Limited.

Carlo Italiano

Carlo Italiano is an illustrator and designer, well known for his work with the *Montreal Star.* Childhood memories of the Italian community in Montreal inspired his prize-winning book, *The Sleighs of My Childhood.* The selection describing the Feast of St. Antony was written especially for *Hooray For Today!* © 1979 by Carlo Italiano.

Bess Kaplan

Bess Kaplan is a well-known Winnipeg author and former editor of *The Jewish Post.* Her first two novels, *Corner Store* and *Malke, Malke,* have been warmly received in both Canada and the United States. The Hanukkah selection is adapted from an unpublished short story entitled "A Chanukah Memoir" © 1979 by Bess Kaplan.

Myrna Kostash

Myrna Kostash is a prominent writer whose work appears regularly in *Saturday Night.* Besides frequent articles in Canadian magazines, she has written several stories and essays. The excerpt is from *All of Baba's Children,* reprinted by permission of Hurtig Publishers.

Jean Little

Jean Little is one of Canada's leading children's authors. Her most recent work, *Listen For the Singing,* was given the Canada Council Prize for Children's Literature in 1978. The excerpt is from her first award-winning book, *Mine For Keeps,* reprinted by permission of Little, Brown and Company Limited, Toronto.

Leslie McFarlane

Leslie McFarlane (1903-1977) is probably best known as the writer of the Hardy Boys series, under the pseudonym Franklin W. Dixon, but he also wrote many novels, articles and radio and TV plays under his own name. The selection is adapted from excerpts taken from *Groups* (Gage Educational Publishing Limited) and *The Last of the Great Picnics* (The Canadian Publishers, McClelland and Stewart Limited, Toronto). The two excerpts are combined and reprinted by permission of the publishers.

Susanna Moodie

Susanna Moodie (1803-1885) was one of Upper Canada's most prolific authors. Her books and articles provide a rich description of pioneer life. The excerpt from *Life in the Clearings* is reprinted by permission of The Macmillan Company of Canada Limited.

Andy O'Brien

Andy O'Brien is well known for his weekly columns in the *Montreal Standard* and the *Toronto Star.* He has also written several sports books, the most recent dealing with the Olympics. The Grey Cup selection was originally published in the *Weekend Magazine,* November 25, 1978. It is reprinted by permission of the author.

Pitseolak

Pitseolak is a distinguished Inuit artist. She describes the "old ways" in her book *Pitseolak: Pictures out of my Life,* (based on recorded interviews by Dorothy Eber), Oxford University Press. The excerpt is adapted and reprinted by permission of Dorothy Eber.

Horst Schmid

While he was responsible for culture in the Alberta government, Horst Schmid did a great deal to promote the arts in his province. He is currently the Alberta Minister of State for Economic Development and International Trade. The Oktoberfest selection was written especially for *Hooray For Today!* © 1979 by Horst Schmid.

Miyuki Tanobe

A widely travelled Japanese artist, Miyuki Tanobe settled in Québec in 1971. Her warm feelings for the province and its people are captured in her award-winning book *Québec je t'aime I love you.* The excerpt is from *Québec je t'aime I love you,* © 1976, reprinted by permission of Tundra Books.

Traditional

This version of the traditional West Indian song *Tinga-lay-o* was created by Sharon Hampson, Lois Lilienstein and Bram Morrison of Pachyderm Music for their children's record *One Elephant, Deux Eléphants.* The first verse was written by children, the third and fourth by a music consultant, and the fifth by a participant at the Mariposa Folk Festival. They are reprinted by permission of Bram Morrison.

Kerry Wood

Kerry Wood is a freelance writer of Scottish background who grew up on a ranch in Alberta. His books include a collection of stories about cowboys, three volumes on natural history and a novel, *Samson's Long Ride.* The excerpt, from *Something to Remember,* is reprinted by permission of Gage Educational Publishers.

Fran
Newman

Claudette
Boulanger

Fran Newman and Claudette Boulanger met when Claudette's young daughter became a member of Fran's grade six class. The two became firm friends, and the result is a two-volume tribute to Canadian children for The International Year of the Child: *Sunflakes & Snowshine* and *Hooray For Today!*

Originally a Westerner, in 1970 Fran followed her air force husband east, where she now lives with her family ("five kids, three cats, two dogs, three horses and fourteen chickens") on a farm near Frankford, Ontario. An enthusiastic and creative teacher, she brought her personal love for poetry to the classroom. The children's encouraging response persuaded her to begin writing verses of her own.

Recognizing a similar sensitivity to the world of childhood in the art of her friend, Fran proposed a "seasons" book that would capture the typical Canadian child's activities throughout the year. Claudette was delighted with the idea, and together they produced *Sunflakes & Snowshine*. As soon as their seasons book was finished, the two decided that a book of festivals was badly needed and eagerly started work on *Hooray For Today!*

Claudette's interest in art began very early; she remembers frequent complaints from her teachers that she was always drawing when she should have been studying. Her unusual crayon work is particularly appealing to children, and she considers her own three children her best – and harshest – critics. Claudette has had a number of successful shows and has recently won two major awards: a National Award for Cartooning in the Public Interest in 1977, and a 1978 Award of Merit from The Art Director's Club of Toronto for the illustrations from *Sunflakes & Snowshine.*